LET'S CELEBRATE

WINTER

WORLD FESTIVALS

Rhoda Nottridge

Wayland

Other titles in this series include:

Let's Celebrate Spring
Let's Celebrate Summer
Let's Celebrate Autumn

Editor: Deb Elliott
Designer: Helen White

Cover: (top left) The colourful Rio Carnival. (top right) A stall holder dressed as Ebisu, one of the seven gods of fortune, at the new year festival in Tokyo, Japan. (bottom left) Christmas decorations in Germany. (bottom right) Dressing up for Mardi Gras in New Orleans, USA.

Text is based on *Winter Festivals* in the *Seasonal Festivals* series published in 1990.

First published in 1994 by
Wayland (Publishers) Limited
61 Western Road, Hove
East Sussex, BN3 1JD, England

British Library Cataloguing in Publication Data
Nottridge, Rhoda
    Winter – (Let's Celebrate Series)
    I. Title II. Series
    508

ISBN 0 7502 1181 4

Typeset by White Design
Printed and bound by Casterman S.A., Belgium

ROTHERHAM PUBLIC LIBRARIES

This book must be returned by the date specified at the time of issue as the Date Due for Return.

The loan may be extended (personally, by post or telephone) for a further period, if the book is not required by another reader, by quoting the above number

LM1 (C)

CONTENTS

WINTER TIME

In winter time it is cold in many parts of the world. The trees have no leaves and many plants die. Some animals go to sleep for the winter. In many places there is a lot of snow and ice. It can be difficult for people to get to work or school because the roads are covered in snow.

BELOW In Finland, children make candles for a festival in the middle of winter.

ABOVE Some animals grow long coats of wool and stay together to keep warm in the winter.

Farmers have to look after their animals by giving them extra food and places to shelter. There may not be much food because it is too cold for anything to grow.

Winter can be fun, too. There are special sports in cold countries. People can go skiing in the snow. If water is frozen they can go skating on the ice. In some countries it does not get cold in winter.

MIDWINTER FESTIVALS

ABOVE A cake shaped like a wooden log is a part of midwinter celebrations in some countries.

Midwinter is the time in the year when many parts of the world have daylight for only a short time and the nights are very long.

Years ago, in northern Europe, there were torchlit processions and big bonfires in midwinter. People would find a huge log of wood and put it on the bonfire. This was called the yule log. It burned for three days. Then the people kept some of the ash from the log to give them good luck in the new year.

In northern Europe in ancient times people believed in ghosts. They thought that at their midwinter festival, the ghosts of their dead friends and families visited them. In China and some other countries it is still a time to remember the dead. Chinese families invite the ghosts to a special feast and offer gifts to them to keep them happy.

LEFT In Finland, candles are put on family graves in midwinter to remember the dead.

CHRISTMAS TIME

Christmas is a festival which celebrates the birth of Jesus Christ. In many parts of the world, Christians celebrate the 25 December each year. In cold countries Christmas became a part of the old midwinter celebrations. In some countries, such as Australia or South Africa, December is in the middle of the summer so it is warm at Christmas time.

BELOW In Sweden there is a special Christian festival on 13 December for Saint Lucia. One girl is chosen to be the Lucia queen, and there is a procession where the girls carry candles and wear long, white dresses.

ABOVE During the Roman festival of Saturnalia everyone had a merry time. Some of the old customs became part of the Christian festival of Christmas.

In ancient times, the Romans had a festival called Saturnalia which they celebrated in December. The Christians chose to celebrate the birth of Christ during Saturnalia. The Romans became Christians and so they started to celebrate the Christmas festival instead of Saturnalia. However, some of the old celebrations were carried on in the new Christian festival. The custom of having parties and decorating homes with holly and ivy goes back to Saturnalia.

CHRISTMAS CUSTOMS

At Christmas time there are many traditions which are carried out every year. Some of them have been going on for hundreds of years. Putting a piece of mistletoe up is a custom that began before Christmas was a Christian festival. It comes from a time in Britain when mistletoe was a very important plant to an ancient people called the Druids.

BELOW *People celebrate Christmas in many parts of the world. This building is decorated for Christmas in Hong Kong.*

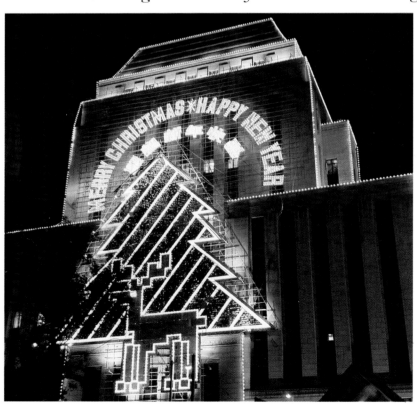

ABOVE Every year children send letters to Santa Claus. They hope he will make their wishes come true.

Some customs come from the old midwinter festivals of northern Europe. In ancient stories, a god called Odin visited the earth in midwinter. He rewarded good people and punished bad people. When Christianity spread, Saint Nicholas replaced Odin in the stories. Saint Nicholas brought gifts to good children. In the Netherlands, Saint Nicholas was called Sinterklaas. Nowadays he is called Santa Claus in many parts of the world.

PERUVIAN FESTIVALS

ABOVE Some people in Peru dress in the kind of clothes the Incas used to wear during the Inti festival.

In Peru in South America there was a midwinter festival in ancient Inca times. For three days people watched the sun rise and honoured their sun god called Inti.

Today some Peruvians continue these old traditions.

They dress in the kind of clothes the Incas used to wear. These are brightly coloured and decorated with patterns of stripes, squares, circles and other shapes.

Many years ago some Spanish people arrived in Peru and ruled the country. The Spanish people were Christians. They changed the time of the old Inca festival. They made it the day of a Christian festival called Corpus Christi.

BELOW *The festival celebrations for Inti are held in a place called Sacsahuaman. The Incas once lived there.*

PONGAL FESTIVAL

LEFT Families clean their homes and draw colourful patterns on the floor for the Pongal festival.

In Tamil Nadu in southern India there is a special three-day festival called Pongal. It is held in January. People give thanks for the rice that has grown and the rain that has helped it to grow.

On the first day of the festival people take special gifts to the temples. One of the gifts is a statue of a horse made out of clay. This is often brightly painted and can be nearly one metre tall.

On the second day of the Pongal festival, gifts of sweets made from fruit and new rice are taken to the temple. These gifts give thanks to the gods for the sun that helps the rice grow. Later the sweets are shared out between everyone.

On the last day of the festival the people give thanks to the cattle, which have worked all year pulling the ploughs across the land so the rice can grow.

BELOW Cattle are special animals in India. During Pongal they are decorated to thank them for their work.

NEW YEAR

For many people, 1 January is the beginning of a new year. The evening before the new year starts is called new year's eve. Many people have parties. In the first minutes after midnight on 31 December, they all wish each other a happy new year.

BELOW In Moscow in Russia, people gather together in candlelight to celebrate the new year.

ABOVE Lights and bonfires are often a part of winter festivals. These lanterns have been put on a hill to bring light to the new year in a Japanese city.

In Scotland, new year's eve is called Hogmanay. There are bonfires, feasts and special songs. The first person to enter the house after midnight can bring good luck. They should carry a piece of coal or bread as a gift. The coal means the family will not be cold and the bread means that they will not go hungry in the year ahead.

CHINESE NEW YEAR

LEFT In London many Chinese people gather together and have colourful processions to start the Chinese new year.

Since ancient times the Chinese have used a calendar based on the position of the moon and the sun to decide on the time of the new year. The date for new year changes every year. It is some time between the middle of January and the middle of February.

In China, the government decided the new year should be on 1 January. It is Chinese people living in other countries who celebrate the ancient new year.

ABOVE People put lettuce and money in a red envelope on pieces of string. When the dragon dances up to their shop he takes the gifts in his mouth. This makes the dragon happy and brings good luck.

New year is a big family festival. In every country where there are a lot of Chinese people, they gather together to celebrate. One important part of the festival is the dragon dance. Inside a dragon or lion costume a group of men make the creature move like a real animal. It dances around to the banging of a drum and brings good luck.

CHINESE CUSTOMS

A week before the new year, Chinese families come together for a special event to honour the god of the kitchen. Some Chinese people believe that the god will go up to the Emperor of Heaven and tell him what the family have thought and said over the year. The lips on a picture of the god are covered in honey. This means that the god will only say sweet things about the family.

BELOW Fireworks are an important part of the new year celebrations in Hong Kong.

ABOVE This model of a dragon is part of a Chinese new year procession.

On the evening before new year, the kitchen god returns to the family. The god is welcomed home with a big feast. There are lots of special foods during the new year celebrations. Some special cakes have messages inside them bringing luck. Some food is set out for the ghosts of each family so that they will also be happy in the year ahead.

JAPANESE NEW YEAR

In Japan, new year is celebrated on 1 January. Many Japanese people have a festival which is a mixture of two religions – Buddhism and Shinto.

On new year's eve, Japanese Buddhists think about all the good things that happened to them in the last year. Then they think about how they need to keep good things in their lives in the year ahead. At midnight the temple bells ring 108 times. This is a special number for Buddhists. It means that the new year can begin without evil.

BELOW Special decorations are put up to keep away bad luck in the year ahead.

LEFT *This man is wearing special clothes which he hopes will bring him and his business good luck in the new year.*

Shinto families prepare for the new year by cleaning their homes on 13 December. They put pieces of bamboo in their homes. Over the door a decoration of paper and rice straws keeps out bad luck.

On new year's day families give each other gifts and promise to forgive anyone who has upset them. There is a special meal with black beans to bring good health and seaweed to bring happiness.

CARNIVAL TIME

Carnival is a Christian celebration. It takes place just before Lent. Lent is the forty days before Easter. During Lent Christians usually give up a food or something they like, so carnival is their last chance to feast before Lent. There is usually a big procession during carnivals. In Spain, Portugal and the Caribbean there are big parties and parades with giant puppets.

BELOW During Mardi Gras in the USA some people dress up in costume and wear masks.

ABOVE Both people and their cars are decorated to take part in the Mardi Gras procession.

People throw flowers at each other as part of the fun in Italy and France. The French call the carnival Mardi Gras. French people who moved to the USA carried on this festival. In New Orleans, Mardi Gras is now a huge celebration.

RIO CARNIVAL

ABOVE This is one of the enormous floats in the Rio parade. As soon as one year's carnival is finished people start to plan the next one.

In Rio de Janeiro in Brazil the carnival celebrations are world famous. There are special groups called samba schools in each area of the city. Each year, they prepare for the carnival and hope to be the best samba school and win prizes at the carnival.

There are huge floats for the parade. Some are covered in gold and silver decorations. Others are beautifully carved out of wood. Each samba school has a queen who has a splendid costume and sits on the float.

The music for carnival is called samba. Each group has a band and dancers who practise special new movements. The dancing carries on at street parties all over the city.

BELOW Dancers wear wonderful costumes and have special competitions for the best groups.

In some countries snow is a part of winter. Although it is cold people can enjoy winter games. In Quebec in Canada there is a special festival during the snowy season. People carve statues out of ice. It is so cold that the statues stay frozen. In northern Japan people also make ice statues.

LEFT This carving in Austria is made out of ice. It stays frozen because it is so cold.

ABOVE These huge models of a snowman and the sun are part of the winter ice festival in Quebec in Canada.

There is a snow festival in Japan that starts at the beginning of February. Children build igloos out of blocks of snow. Inside the igloo there is a special place lit with candles. At this place the children give thanks to the god who brings water to the earth.

GLOSSARY

ancient Something that is very old or that happened a long time ago.

carved To be cut out of wood or ice.

costumes Special clothes which people wear when they are dressing up for a festival or special party.

customs Habits which are passed down from older people to younger people.

evil Something that is very bad or harmful.

floats Lorries which are specially decorated and carry people in a parade.

igloo A kind of house built out of blocks of snow.

log The main branch or trunk of a tree that has been stripped of any other branches.

mistletoe A kind of green plant with white berries.

procession A group of people who move along together during a festival or special event.

plough A tool used for turning over the earth before planting seeds.

shelter A place to keep warm and dry away from bad weather.

statue A model of a human or animal made out of a material such as wood or stone.

traditions Customs that have been carried on for many years.

BOOKS TO READ

Chinese Spring Festival by Ming Tsow (Evans, 1988)
Christmas by Tim Wood (A&C Black, 1991)
Christmas Customs by Dennis Miller (Ladybird, 1988)
Dat's New Year by Linda Smith (A&C Black, 1985)
In Winter by Ruth Thomson (Watts, 1993)
Poems for Winter selected by Robert Hull (Wayland, 1990)
Winter by Ruth Thomson (Watts, 1989)

Picture acknowledgements
The publishers would like to thank the following for allowing their pictures to be reproduced in this book:

Barnaby's Picture Library 10, 19, 21; Cephas 28; Eye Ubiquitous cover (top right, Frank Leather), 17, 23; Hutchison Library 12, 13, 14, 15, 16; The Mansell Collection 9; Photri 4, 6, 7, 11, 24, 29; Tony Stone Worldwide 5, 18, 20, 26, 27; Topham 8, 22, 25; Zefa cover (top left, Veiga Leal), (bottom left, Rosenfeld), (bottom right). All artwork is by Maggie Downer.

INDEX